This is me…

This is me since yesterday

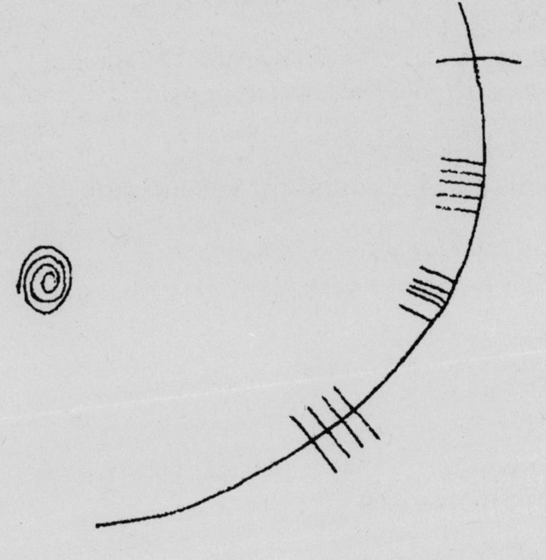

Alexandra Leggat

Coach House Books

Cover Art: Untitled (1994) by Anne O'Callaghan
Slate incised, gold leaf and acrylic paint [23″ x 19″]

CANADIAN CATALOGUING IN PUBLICATION

Leggat, Karen Alexandra, 1964
This is me since yesterday

Poems.
ISBN 1-55245-036-8

1. Title

PS8573.E461716T44 1999 C8!!'.54 C98-931505-3
PR9199.3.L43T44 1999

Now I realize
it's not so much where I'm going
but where I'm returning to that scares me

here I go again
straight into me

Providence

Here I stand, so close to young
yet years away from when it all began

no matter how I change
these little-girl-untamed-eyes won't close

and all my reflecting
fails to enlighten me

I'm unable to continue
without resolving where I've come from

but how many times can I go back
before I'm swallowed by my past

do I have to take this
right back to the womb

sorry Mom, I should have called
I know you weren't expecting to be expecting me again

Like Bugs

Some days I feel like I'm sitting in a city alley
catching flies on my tongue
tapping my foot to an old song
trying to drown out a nagging thought
that's buzzing around my head like flies

and I wish I could sense danger
like an animal
and run like anger
when a bottle becomes a blanket

I have a Marc Bolan fear of cars
of anything too futile and metallic
that could drive me to my grave
of porcelain boys who'll break me
in a clumsy attempt to keep themselves unscathed

and I wish I could sense danger
like an animal
and run like anger
when a bottle becomes a blanket

I wonder why a thing like God is strange to me

I wouldn't know it if I tripped over it
and I wish that I would
that I could
catch it on my tongue
like a bug

Home

Somewhere in between Chelsea
and the pages of my New York Times

I feel England
in me, like we'd never come untied

a familiar sensibility
that's molded my mind

the soil I've grown up treading on
still feels strange beneath my soles

but from the sound of my voice
who'd know

Botticelli Angel

She insisted on growing up every two weeks
on having no page left unturned
no road untravelled
no words left unsaid
and nothing
would slip through her fingers – more than once

She found daytime was fine
in small doses
Everything
in moderation
At night she could exist unnoticed
and float amidst the stars

She said, 'I know there's someone out there for me
waiting for me.
If you see him
tell him I'll be late.

Tell him
I've been framed.'

Lucy

It's a bore being and breathing and the like
when still you can't do so many things

It's a chore being and wondering and the like
when feeling out loud can lead to so many problems

It's a trial being and thinking and the like
when nature has so many laws

Angelica

My eyes cry from the heart, she says
perched upon a neon altar
in the church of the New Constitution
located on the outskirts of Texas

Some day I'll be somewhere, she says
far from here and the stockade that locks me to my fate
I've seen tomorrow, oh yes, and I've kissed its feet
so it owes me

the light fades from her bluish, grayish, reddish eyes
embers leap from her palms as they burn with regret
another layer of skin sacrificed to the god of
why did I ever do that

Silenced and silent she drops to her knees
thoughts are the placards of the soul, she says
that clothe the skeleton of the redeemer
so here I am, all dressed up and nowhere to go

Icing and The Cake

Blonde ambition can be a little wobbly
but when it stumbles
it stumbles onto a good thing

Truly, truly, truly
a paper plate existence has longevity
in the recycling age

There is life beneath the sea
beneath its rippling, rolling, crashing face

A superior life
able to breathe under water
under pressure
under all of you

This is it...

I'm thinking about life's injustices
and the absence of something in everything

as the eyes of the world
look down upon me pupil-less

heroes fall like toddlers
once you get to know them

everyone's human
that's the worst of it

a little left unknown
is the best thing

nothing sacred
nothing sanctimonious

and tomorrow
albeit

is just another day

Ian

for Joy Division

All catastrophe is wide
like the Grand Canyon
the echo hangs
longer than a dead man at the end of a rope
all limbs raggedy before the blood goes cold
and everything turns blue in you
and the cry still lingers in nothing but space

daffodils and bubbles can make you smile
after he's cut down and the empty kitchen is a blessing
footsteps come and go in you
but whose legs they belonged to escapes you
and there are no bubbles in the whole of heaven
that can change the end of him
and daffodils don't bloom till spring
and the ice and the gray and the depth of your breath
confirm its still January

all his secrets slept with strangers
and laughed a public image laugh
but nothing was funny
and nothing was said

when all his prettiest songs forgot their words
and no chorus was worth repeating
when the lights went out at Barton Street
and the captain's knot sailed him
the easy way on

The Reverie

Time reveals thoughts through thinning skin
eternity is tissue
peril's a shot of scotch
at night
alone
when the last bulb burns out
and snow creeps in through the cracks in your head

the map is changing
the ground keeps moving under foot
you're never left musing in the same place twice
what calamity
poor reverie
left hanging
without an end

La Dee Da, La Dee Da

there were so many close calls
long distance calls
to the one you look up to
and down on when he's not around

and it wasn't the Toradal that would've killed you
that really strong pain killer
that couldn't even quell your headaches

it wasn't the bottle of AC&Cs
or the Javex beneath the sink

but

the monotony of trying

Ton Of Bricks

If tired is the end
then I'm ending
heavy lidded

loaded
like I'd swallowed a hundred bullets
and shot my mouth off

all I've got to show for it is tired

limbs heavy – an elephant's
a hundred me's could fit into an elephant
but the elephant has fit into me

I lumber to bed
and fall into sleep

five minutes pass
and the next day's knocking pestilently
on my skull

But I'm not ready for more
I'm not ready

And if it were easy
I'd be dead
but I'm dead tired

it's the best I can do

Subconscious

Last night I dreamt
I was dying

in a hospital bed
surrounded by loved ones

a friend walked in
leaned over me

and said
I had no idea that you were dying

what are you dying of
I looked at him and said

boredom

then, I died

No Mercy

catastrophic, it should have been
the whole world disintegrated beneath our feet
and it didn't matter

like the time
we accidentally split the praying mantis in half
and both halves lived on
independent of one another
and probably a lot happier

catastrophic, it should have been
they closed the gates to heaven
just as I was steppin' in

Hmmm

I used to think of a black and white existence
it is not me that is small
but life itself

these are different eyes looking at the same scene
all told and not left listening
it's a rare sight

I used to think it was
each day
pulled to a sunken chest

Chapter 1

the tomorrow books are waiting
it's winter now and there's
time to be spent productively
indoors and upright

thank heaven for seasons
thank whom and whatever
for your ninth life
at least you think it must be up there
by now

too many chances
wasted in unconsciousness
if you remembered the riots
would you have bothered to fight

you see your breath in the early morning
you'll see it again tonight
the good thing about winter
is there's proof that you're still alive

The Coldest Day

The way the city streets look in winter
solemn & salty & gray
adds a new dimension to the place
reveals its alter-ego
the flip side – filthy, desperate & temperamental

and sometimes beyond my window
everything looks so frozen
that if I took a hammer to it
the whole neighbourhood would smash into pieces

and what would be there, if anything
the center of the universe?
another neighbourhood?
Spring?

there's so much to be said for winter
even its little things leave a big impression
like snowflakes, frozen sentiments
the hammer I'm left holding
at the end of the coldest day

Life Sinks

like empty pools
the hollow lies
in the tearless stare of Virginia Woolf's eyes

Melancholy Baby

I'm waving at the aluminum bird in vain
as you sit nervously in its belly

I walk away when it disappears
behind a Hindenburg-like cloud
and for a moment I wonder if that means anything

a neon sign beckons from the side of the road
two swinging cowboy boots
and a pair of blue words – Cold Beer

I take a Gennesee and peruse the juke box
I should play something happy
but choose Daniel instead

and I feel like I'm in the film *Paris, Texas* or *Fool for Love*
and Harry Dean Stanton's about to walk through the door
and Sam Shepard or Dennis Hopper's with him
'cause that's the kind of joint this is

and I'd pull up a chair and ask for a cigarette
and be some kind of melancholy baby
as you soar above me into your new life

Pints

it could have been the dead of winter
the cold uneven evenings
that threw my timing off

the night is unending
and there were days when that was fine
but blackness is blinding

forget that I forgot you
those days when you said I needed you most
it's not easy being generous in poor times

over another cold drink
your face in every bubble
the song on the radio knows

the walking away wasn't hard
sitting here thinking about you
only confirms it

Cropped Up in San Francisco

when I knew you last
your golden baby hair
swayed like my breezy thoughts about you
and the great life you were leading
south of the border

sun-kissed skin's a far cry
from the rice and bean-curd complexion
that's stretched across your hairless head
and slouching in front of me at our point of reunion
this is what Zen has done for you?

your California crazed-up fantasies
can only be cashed in in L.A. you say
and you lead me to your one-eyed girlfriend
who's been baking bread since 5 AM
and just informed you she's pregnant
and happy about it

I play Pac-Man in the café
at the end of Haight Street
and think about Seal Rock and Alcatraz
eating jelly beans

one for each of life's little religions
you're somewhere else
on your knees with your eyes closed

This Friend

You said the vacation restored you.
You saw coyotes
and found birch bark.
That was the highlight.
No, your husband was the highlight –
you said as an afterthought.

Two days in Sudbury
and the world changes for you.
A piece of a tree's shredded skin and
the world changes for you.
Some slag.
Slag? I have to ask.
It's the dregs of the nickel mines, you explain.

And you'll chip away all night at the bark
like you chipped away all day
on the piece of coral I brought you from the Bahamas.
And I wish I had more to chip away on
than my very own bones.

Copyright 1964

for Nick Drake

You were a new realm of things
eyes that wouldn't close in the dark
and a mind   boundless   an ocean
when standing on a beach at the crack of dawn

your sloping shoulders
carried every day of your life since birth
you could've been so tall and hopeful

and I think of you today   while standing
on Brighton's   almost   clean sand
a careless rain   ruining any chance of forgiveness

behind me   an ice cream van waits by the empty pier
undaunted   its jingle clamors through the weather
and it's then   I realize
nothing is boundless

Jacked-Off

if it weren't for the

cadillacs
hot tubs
portable telephones
televisions
toilets

love on a rope

two-bit
jerk-jobs
dealing
Tijuana low-down-philosophy-in-a-cup
not just adding water

pay for

a fortune
a forte
foreplay

foul play's
good play
today

this could be a fine, fine time

See Jane Run

another book ingested
and despite all that she consumes
she still doesn't grow

then she thinks it must be something
in her genes because
even her hair doesn't grow

for years she hasn't been cutting it
in general that is
you know   not making it

she's been considering
going to a body-piercing salon
to have a steel bar put across her brow

to protect her from
all the brick walls
she keeps on running into

Portable Demons

I found the ghost of Dorothy Parker
in an old movie house in Times Square
I approached her with condolences
and slowly coerced her out of there

I walked her to a warm home
and fed her food a mother would
I laid her in a fresh made bed
and sat by her side while she slept

through broken dreams
she spoke of carefree moments
with men she'd never met
she threw her arms in the air
at the irony of dying all her life
and still never having left

I held her in my shaky arms
knowing that if she woke to find me
cradling her like a baby
she'd cackle at our weakness
and push me bitterly away

I awoke to the ghost of Dorothy Parker
eating Corn Flakes in my backyard
the morning paper ripped to shreds
by her cutting retorts
about the hapless writing in print today
and I knew
she was here to stay

The Neglected Dead

As you turn over in the night
in your sleep
in your death state
wrapped in warm bed clothes
and the arms of another
possibly

as you lie nestled
within the safety of four walls
protected
from the elements
from the negligence
of night

souls huddle beneath your window
draped in abandonment

High Tide

There are two men talking.

One says, 'What does your wife do?'

The other says, 'She was a poet.'

'Was?'

'Yes.

One day she threw herself in the wash,

then hung herself

to dry.'

For Sylvia Plath:
Jamaica Plain

and simple there never was
through too clever eyes

a leafless tree
inhaling spring's other blossoms

not wondering why
it was different

this was natural
life wasn't

Radiate Her

The radiator never stops pounding
the heart stops pounding
where's the justice in that
why don't we get to choose our own plumbing

I want to be hot like a radiator
I don't care if I bang and creak
if I have to be bled to give off heat

I just want to be sturdy
and exude warmth

Pay No Mind

Cadillac bound
across the great divide
my wings will save me
when I'm gassed-out in a cold place
flying across icebergs
small obstructions
temporarily waylaid
in the frozen fogginess of ambition
I can wait for an itinerary
from a major airline
or I can pick up and go
land on my feet at the foot
of a new friend
who buys me a coffee
for a poem
I give him a short one
so as not to drain his attention span
I can tell by his roving eyes
it's low
I can take a bus to a small town
and tell a poetic lie
about love and life and dogs
and I can get a laugh for a good line

I can travel across the entire world
with a suitcase packed full of
firmly pressed metaphors
and still not get anywhere in your mind

The Arbiter

come she say, he come

    go she say, he go

up and down, like some kind of yo-yo

blow she say, and the wind come

        and blow, he go roly poly down

the road

    he get right back up and wait

                    he got tear in one eye, he

not let it show

        she reel him in like some kind of yo-yo

Crack Down

It's a walk along crazed roads
the ones where women with black eyes
and a handful of teeth
will make love to you for a dollar
to lose this life in orange powder

And the Coffee Times drenched
in men with bullet holes in their cheeks
and tattoos of Tijuana whores on their biceps
eating chocolate glazed doughnuts in between drags

And these men know the pummeled women
strolling the streets
maybe they were the bruisers
or maybe they're the saviors on rainy nights
when tattooed arms are the only ones open for free

Dexterous

my friend plays saxophone
in the subway
makes loose change and
makes loose living seem so easy
he's got bohemian girlfriends
pierced noses with little gems in them
that twinkle in the dark
he keeps them bi-weekly
so many underground love tickets
swept onto the tracks
invariably picking one up
and taking a ride to the other side of town
where the rumble of engines is always escaping something

he comes home early when the birds get up
crawls lonesome into his bed
dream material brewing
like the coffee I'll be saving
to have with him
when he wakes
and tells me about the night
about the money
dropped in the horn case

about rich woman who wink at him and sometimes
pay in phone numbers
and I think
blowing the tune nightly's
gotta take some pair of lungs

This is me since yesterday

Didn't I write something on the back of an envelope
last night on the tramcar
going home tired and full of ale
Didn't I swear this is the last time
I'll ride home lonely on a week night
Didn't I dream that dream
I was mobile on four chrome wheels
sitting comfy in the '57 T-Bird body – yellow and white

Or is this another memory misplaced
a day or two too late
It could be Cleveland and I thought it was Texas
and now I don't know where I am or where I was going
All I know is I spent my last coin to board this machine
and it's taking me to all the wrong places

Didn't I wonder when I walked past the fire station
I'd never noticed it reeks of smoke
it never dawned on me
the engines bring home remnants
of the damage they put out

Didn't I think my Buffalo shoes
were making more noise on the sidewalk
than all the soldiers I could imagine
Didn't I hate the way my travels echoed through the night
confirming this town's emptiness

Or is this another memory misplaced
a time or two too late
This could be an old life
or it could be that new one I sneered at the thought of
Doubting that there could ever be life
after death after death after death

Didn't I look into your eyes through the grass
and say I was sorry

When The Dream Wakes

there's a north wind blows after sunrise
like your breath running from this day
you're a million miles away
from where you want to be
from oceans and castles

you look across the sky
at its white, billowy silhouettes
of mythical creatures carrying rain
and know they're the most harmless thing
you'll come across all day

the tea gets poured
feet rest on a stool
the paper's still open to the page
with the German artist's out-of-focus painting
the one that inspired you at the art gallery
the day you walked away from it
knowing you'd found a new favourite artist
one you hadn't been brought up to love

you know tonight will be swirling
with your friends' excitement
about their books just out and coming out
about the job they'd found under the mat this morning
that promises to take them around the world for a good buck
and you'll be happy for them
like you always are

like they are for you
when success unpredictably goes to bed with you
on a good night

when a dream you'd concocted breathes life into you
you into it
your only symbiotic relationship
and you'll leave them just around midnight
feeling their sympathetic eyes upon you
and you'll wonder if this is what Dorothy went through
trying to explain to her family
that there really is a place called Oz

The A Train

taking the subway to Flatbush
a Camel light between your teeth
and a thought or two between your ears

vent at your feet
blowing yesterday's air
up into your face

and you were so afraid you'd forget
what yesterday felt like

Not Spoken Softly

into the once again – all over again
a little left up and its right back down
what may came
and it meant it

if at all there'll be consequences
it's inconsequential now
a foot in the mouth is a habit
a foot in somebody else's mouth is a shame

it's a shake of the head
and a hand-slapped brow
to a hum diddly dum
until it happens again

Trans Spired

I gave up my body
    in the form of a seasoned locomotive
it was old
    it was tired
it was time to be retired

I gave it up
I gave it up
it went

I gave up my body
    in the form of a '76 Ford Galaxie 500
it was old
    it was tired
it was time to be re-tired

spirit walks regardless
spirit walks even

    without it

For Arthur Miller

Arthur Arthur
Did you ever think
on your thought-letting walks across
      the Brooklyn bridge
that one day you'd be accused of harboring
      communist sympathies
sharing life with Marilyn Monroe
or commiserating with Clark Gable in Nevada
on the set of one of the greatest films to hit the screen
and did you know then that you were a misfit too

But everything that you stepped into
      seemed to fit regardless
and everything that faced you you took on
then carried on naturally
like the trees you planted in Connecticut
that have grown to be sixty feet tall
and you are in my mind just as rooted

Arthur Arthur
when you look back as you must do
of all the lives that you've created
is it Roslyn who waves most lovingly and full of pride
back at you

Lost Weekend In Brooklyn

You wait by the window for an ounce of redemption
to stroll by
and you wait and you wait

The sun falls and gets back up again
and you've slept without realizing you'd slept

The bed says that you have
and the chunk of time that's passed

with hope, your head's pulled up by your neck
and your gaze thrown back out the window

Nothing's waiting
Nothing's changed
Nothing is forgotten

Thanks for the Memories

The Science magazine says it's only natural,

'emotions or feelings are conscious products
of unconscious processes… Emotional experiences
are the result of
triggering systems of behavioral adaption
that have been preserved
by evolution.'

Mice have proven that emotional memories
can be removed
by removing part of the brain.
That fear can be removed by a scalpel.

Then and only then can one forget.

Moved

I came and went
came and went
inching through
on blistered feet
straw hat keeping away the sun
a lollipop between my lips
for a taste of something sweet

low down
came the night dreams
all tattered ends
peopled with one-time friends
too long gone to remember names
to put fingers on
to even want to have crowding dream time

the little things still unpacked
because the smallest things don't fit just anywhere
and the one room's done
so I'll live there for now
and ignore the rest of the house
because too much space is like too much company
when you're tired

laughter comes rumbling from the desert
a rabid tumbleweed
thinks it's time to roll on
held in tight by shrinking stomach muscles far too long
but a good laugh doesn't last till the sun comes up

like it used to
at slumber parties
when I was underaged and undernourished
in ways that were never meant to be funny anyway

and anyway it's Easter
but chocolate doesn't excite me anymore
Jesus isn't any closer to resurrection
the bird in the pinetree's whistling Dixie
reminiscing about the South
how it would be fine
if I could unlock the door from the inside
and get out

Lo

you came through water like a dorsal fin
it was too much trouble
to keep your head above it
so you dove in and stayed

it's not the lack of air that's strange
but the silence
how it comforts you
and lures you further down

and when the sun beats through the surface
it's warmer than what you've ever felt from love
it's not absolution – being under
but it's home

In Retrospect

Potted thoughts flowered once

into gardens of content

As a child I glided through life

heaven sent

Picture perfect but slightly bent

Epilogue

And You Are America
Giant
Overflowing
Plates Of Food
You are

Typeset in Palatino and printed at the Coach House on bpNichol Lane, April, 1999.

Editor for the press: Victor Coleman

To read the online version of this text and other titles from Coach House Books, or to order any of our titles, visit our website:

www.chbooks.com

To add your name to our e-mailing list, write:

mail@chbooks.com

Toll-free:
1 800 367 6360

Coach House Books
401 Huron Street (rear) on bpNichol Lane
Toronto, Ontario M5S 2G5